STRONG WRITING

RICHARD A. SCHWARTZ, Ph.D.

richardschwartzphd@gmail.com | writeword.weebly.com

STRONG WRITING

RICHARD A. SCHWARTZ, Ph.D.

richardschwartzphd@gmail.com | writeword.weebly.com

STRONG WRITING

Copyright © 2011 by Richard Alan Schwartz
All rights reserved. No part of this book shall be reproduced or transmitted in any form or by any means, electric, mechanical, magnetic, photographic, including photocopying, recording, or by any information retrieval system, without prior written permission of the author. Although every precaution has been taken in preparation of this book, the publisher and author assume no responsibility for errors or omissions. Neither is any liability assumed for damage resulting from the use of information contained herein.

ISBN: 978-1-105-17934-1

http://www.lulu.com/product/paperback/strong-writing/18874107

DEDICATION

This book is dedicated to all the teachers and professors who, over the years, helped me develop and hone my writing skills.

CONTENTS

CHAPTER 1	Disciplined Thinking	8
CHAPTER 2	Purpose	16
CHAPTER 3	The Readers	22
CHAPTER 4	Organization Part I: Business Applications	32
CHAPTER 5	Organization Part II: Academic Essays	54
CHAPTER 6	Grammar	71
CHAPTER 7	Style	94
CHAPTER 8	Proofreading	104

CHAPTER ONE
DISCIPLINED THINKING

I taught university-level English classes for over 35 years and have read literally tens of thousands of student essays. I have also published seven academic books and worked as a computer programmer for a major utility, where I learned the importance of clear, easy-to-follow documentation and inter-office communications. In addition to the continuous stream of undergraduate papers I corrected, I also directed numerous Master's degree theses. But even though I taught courses at every level from freshman English to a graduate-level thesis-writing workshop, invariably I found myself always pointing to the same basic problems in my students' analytical writing. These were also the same problems I encountered in the business environment: the need to be clear about the purpose of the essay or business report, to have a strong sense of who the readers will be and how best to communicate with them, to formulate a precise central thesis that articulates the core idea of the essay, to develop that thesis effectively around main supporting points that are themselves developed within well structured paragraphs, and to construct precise, concise, dynamic sentences. Although these skills are crucial to effective writing, they are not inherently difficult or complicated. I have written *Strong Writing* as a concise handbook to explain each of these central writing concerns and to demonstrate how to craft incisive, clear, and easy-to-follow analytical essays and reports.

Strong writing impresses not with flourishes and grand statements, but with directness. It is swift and dynamic, laying everything out clearly and getting to the point without extra sentences or words. It is assertive, not tentative; active, not passive. Strong writers, like world-class athletes, perform easily, with power and grace, without wasting a motion, because they know what they are doing and how to do it. They are in complete control.

Writing is literally the physical manifestation of thought, and I have always seen a connection between clear writing and clear thinking. I never feel like I have truly mastered a topic until I have written about it, because writing requires me to put my ideas into very concrete terms and to make very precise claims, which I can then challenge. Only when I have succeeded in putting my ideas into a coherent form that shows how they relate to one another, and when I have chosen words that convey all the subtleties and nuances of my thought, do I feel that I have fully understood my subject. On the other hand, when I have finished refining my ideas and language and can fend off any reasonable challenges to them that I can imagine, then I know I own that topic.

Almost everyone in a business or professional environment will complain that the quality of writing in business communications—memos, letters, reports, and proposals—is often poor. And university professors in every discipline routinely complain about the quality of their students' written work, which often fails to state main points precisely, probe topics deeply, or develop ideas with intellectual rigor. Too often student papers and professional reports fail to articulate their main conclusions adequately or remain focused on them. Sometimes writers "talk around" their subject, making several valid but disconnected points. They fail to demonstrate how these points relate to each other or what they ultimately add up to.

The widespread presence of bad writing in our culture suggests a corresponding widespread presence of bad thinking, or at least incomplete thinking: thinking that does not recognize its own limitations, logical contradictions, and ambiguities. *Undisciplined thinking* may be another way to describe it. In our society we tend to phone or text or tweet instead of develop points in substantial paragraphs; to watch instead of read; to understand data in terms of facts and statistics, not sentences and paragraphs; and to take multiple choice and short answer tests instead of essay exams. Whatever benefits this general movement away from the written word may bring, they come at the price of the mental discipline that strong writing cultivates. Since that mental discipline is not often developed in our other activities to the same extent as in writing, it is understandable that our professional and academic communities claim many citizens who are undisciplined, or partially disciplined thinkers, even at some of the highest ranks. So, the most basic cause for bad writing is undisciplined thinking. Writers who do not really know what they want to say, or who do not see the inconsistencies and ambiguities in their thoughts, are unlikely to write crisp, direct prose or to develop their ideas coherently.

When you look at your own writing and see that it does not go anywhere, that the thoughts seem jumbled, and even the simplest instructions feel awkward, it is a good idea to be honest with yourself and ask if you really understand what you are trying to say. Being honest with yourself, telling yourself truthfully both when you do and do not fully understand what you want to say, is crucial to disciplined thinking and strong writing.

Moreover, such honesty carries over into other aspects of your life. The same courage and discipline that tells you the paragraph you just re-wrote for the fifth time still is not quite right, despite the fact that you really want it to be, may also tell you that the person you really want to be Mr. or Ms. Right just isn't. And that will save a lot of pain later on. Conversely, when you are as intellectually demanding of yourself as any of your challengers might be, and you are still satisfied with what you have written, then you will feel quite confident that no one is going to shoot you down. And that confidence in your own judgment carries-over into your personal life as well. So, by developing the discipline, rigor, and capacity for self-confrontation that are necessary for writing, you are also making yourself a stronger person, capable of achieving greater self-knowledge. Having the courage to see honestly and acknowledge when you have done well or poorly, then, is essential to becoming a strong person as well as a strong writer. If you do not have it now, such courage is worth cultivating. It comes down to accepting yourself well enough to acknowledge that it is permissible, and certainly inevitable, to make mistakes.

Making mistakes does not make you a bad person or a failure. That should seem like an obvious statement, but many people cannot let themselves see their mistakes because in their mind doing so would make them failures. That condition is not only psychologically unhealthy, it also precludes an honest scrutiny of their own work. Unless we see ourselves and our work honestly, we are not living and writing in the real world of most of our fellow students, professors, colleagues, and co-workers. Consequently, we will be ineffective students and professionals, as well as ineffective writers.

So, if you believe you may routinely blind yourself to your own mistakes, take some time to reflect on that and on whether you won't be happier and better off to seek them out and acknowledge them so you can correct them and prevent them from harming you in the future.

Assuming you have the courage and capacity to recognize your own mistakes if you see them and the commitment to rectify them, then the next step is to learn to see problems more easily and in sharper focus. You can do this simply by questioning yourself: *Is this statement clear? Does it say exactly what I mean, or is it imprecise or awkward or confused?"* If the latter, then ask, *What am I really trying to say?* **This is the single-most important question.** But there are others: *What is the logical connection between these two sentences, or between these two paragraphs, and have I made that connection clear? Have I shown it or merely implied* *it and thereby placed the burden on my reader to figure it out? Was my demonstration adequate for my reader? Is my logic correct, and can I think of anything that would contradict my claims and conclusions?*

By routinely asking yourself these questions and by formulating other ones, you will bring rigor to your thought process, and you will typically discover most of your mistakes and shortcomings before anyone else ever sees them. Moreover, your writing will become more focused and direct and people will perceive you as a strong and very structured thinker.

Challenging yourself honestly on every statement will do all of these things for you. It is a matter of discipline, of making yourself do what you know you need to do. This self confrontation is essential to strong writing, and it is a useful practice for life in general, although there are moments when highly analytic thought is inappropriate, when it can lessen your fun or upset others. These times usually occur during periods of leisure or intimacy. So try to become attuned to what each situation calls for in your writing and in your life.

In summary, undisciplined thinking is the most basic problem for writers. If the underlying thoughts are scattered, incoherent, or poorly defined, or if the sentences do not truly state what the writer is trying to say, then no amount of tinkering with stylistics or addition of graphic illustrations will fix it. Thus rigorous, disciplined thought is the *sine qua non* of strong writing: without it there is nothing. And with it, everything else falls into place. Rigorous thinkers will ultimately hit upon a sound organizational strategy, because they will reject patterns of organization that obscure main points rather than highlight them. Moreover, their words will say exactly what they mean because 1) they truly know what they mean, and 2) they reject words, phrases, and sentences that fail to articulate it precisely.

CHAPTER TWO
PURPOSE

The six most important elements of good writing are knowing why you are writing and what you hope to accomplish from it, understanding your audience, organizing your material logically and in sufficient detail for the purpose, writing grammatically, achieving an effective style, and proofreading your work rigorously. *Strong Writing* centers on these issues.

Most academic and professional writing ultimately is a form of teaching: explaining something to someone who does not already know it. This is true for memoranda, reports, business letters, proposals—virtually any form of business writing—as well as student essays, term papers, Master's theses, and doctoral dissertations. Even if the reader is an expert in the field, approaching the writing as an act of teaching compels you to think about how the reader will respond to each statement, whether the points are clear, and whether each sentence and paragraph ultimately conveys what it should. Moreover, thinking of yourself as a teacher when you write makes the writing experience interactive. Your writing becomes not merely an act of self expression or a neutral presentation of facts; *it is the medium through which you engage other people.* As a writer/teacher you will become more aware of your responsibility to your readers and will recognize that it is your job to make sure your readers can follow what you are saying, because you will experience writing as a three-way interaction among yourself, your subject, and your readers.

People who do not perceive that writing is an act of teaching often experience writing as just a two-way interaction: between themselves and the subject. They place the burden of understanding on the readers and not on themselves; whereas writer/teachers accept the responsibility of conveying information in ways their readers can best understand it. Therefore, never lose sight that the purpose of the writing is not simply to present facts and ideas, but to do so in a way that will have a desired effect on your readers—whether it be to inform them, convince them, or spur them to action. Good teachers and strong writers are also good problem solvers. In a very fundamental way, all writing and teaching is problem solving. And so the basic principles of problem solving apply to good writing.

KNOW THE PURPOSE(S) OF THE TASK

Recall from high school that the first step in the scientific method is to define the problem. So too in writing. What is the purpose of the writing task? What do you hope to achieve by it? This is the first question you should ask yourself before you begin to write anything. Why are you doing it?

The answer may have several dimensions. The reason for writing a report, for example, may be to pass along the executive chain-of-command the findings about some issue, so a senior executive can act responsibly and wisely upon your information. Since you know that an important vice president will be reading this report, another objective of your writing might be to have him or her take notice of you and gain respect for your abilities. And since, if the executives accept your recommendations you will receive a choice assignment, another objective might be to persuade them to decide as you want them to. If these are your ultimate goals, then everything in your report should be directed toward one or more of them, in some capacity. If anything appears in the report that is not somehow directed at these goals, it is irrelevant and should be deleted. Of course, your basic integrity should preclude you from distorting the report to yield improper conclusions, even if those might somehow work to your advantage.

If you are writing a paper for class, you still need to ascertain the purpose of the assignment. The ultimate purpose presumably is to receive an A grade, if grades are your greatest motivation, or to learn as much as possible from the assignment, if your sentiments are loftier. Either case requires you to satisfy the professor's expectations; so you need to ascertain what they are. Does the professor want you to accumulate, synthesize, and present a body of information, without expressing your own thoughts about it? Or should you summarize and respond to other writers' positions, or express your own subjective response to the subject? Each of these writing objectives will result in a different kind of essay.

Once you are clear about what you want your writing to accomplish, then you need to ascertain the best way to do it. First, ask yourself what response you want from your reader. Do you want her to be better informed than before she read your memo or report? Or do you want to convince her to take specific action: to give you a new assignment, or buy a new copy machine, or change the vendor who sells you printer cartridges? Or, for a school paper, do you want your professor to feel you understand the facts of a situation fully and completely? Or do you want to convince the professor that your analysis of the situation is correct? The response you want from your reader should be the focus of your writing.

In most instances, it is best to state your purpose in the first paragraph, with the understanding that everything that follows represents the rationale and supporting data for why that action is a good idea. If your purpose is simply to inform, you should normally state the basic conclusions or more general facts in the first paragraph. The rest of the report will then elaborate on those conclusions or facts.

Some writers are reluctant to present their material this way. They say they want to build to a grand conclusion, that stating the bottom line first will destroy the suspense or interest. If these writers would reconsider the goals for their writing, they would realize that maintaining suspense is not one of them. Suspense is great for novels and screenplays, but busy professionals and professors want to know the bottom line right away. So why make them wait? They might not even be greatly interested in the supporting detail, especially if they trust your judgment. So there is no reason to beat around the bush. Come out immediately and state what you want the reader to do or know. If you are able to make a strong case for that action—and if you practice rigorous, disciplined thinking you should be able to do so—then there is no reason to be shy. State your purpose directly from the beginning.

CHAPTER THREE
THE READERS

Usually disciplined thinking is something we apply to subject matter. For instance, I would base my judgment about what kind of laptop computers my firm should purchase on a rigorous set of questions about each model concerning how well it will serve our needs in comparison to how much it will cost.

But we can also apply disciplined thinking to our readers by trying to understand them. Who are they? What is their level of understanding about the topic? At what level of detail or abstraction should you address them? What do they expect or desire to receive from your report or memo? In what terms, language, and orientation do they perceive things? What would make them want to act in the way you desire? If the reader is a teacher or professor, what, exactly, does he or she want you to demonstrate about your mastery of the subject when you fulfill the assignment?

The trick in strong writing that serves both readers and writers is for the writers to formulate strategies that will satisfy the readers' needs or desires and still accomplish what the writers want. The best way to achieve this is to say what you want to say, but on their terms. This requires you to think about your readers a little before you start writing. Do they know the general background of your topic, or do they need to be filled in? If so, how much detail do they require or desire? What, exactly, do they need to be informed about? Are they familiar with the jargon and specialized terms and concepts you use, or do you need to explain your terms when you first employ them? How will the information you provide be useful to your readers, and can you tailor your presentation in a way that highlights its usefulness? **Anticipating your readers' needs and providing for them are two of the most valuable skills you can develop as a writer.**

For instance, let's say you are a middle manager in the Human Resources Department, and you are writing a report to the head of the department about the results of an on-going experiment with flex-time that the Computing Services Department has been trying. How would you go about analyzing your reader?

First, identify her. She is your department manager. Therefore, she is familiar with the flex-time experiment, because she was involved in setting it up and approving it. This means you will not have to explain what flex-time is or give the details of how the experiment worked. There is no sense in wasting her time and yours by telling her what she already knows. She understands the topic well, and she knows the special in-house jargon associated with it. So you can feel free to refer to basic and secondary issues without explaining them; and you may employ specialized language, because you know that she will know what you are talking about.

Because she is your immediate supervisor and therefore close to you in the corporate hierarchy, you do not have to be strictly formal, unless that is how you otherwise interact. For instance, if she is the only person intended to read your report, you might refer to your co-workers by their first names and employ other insider references.

Finally, since she was the biggest advocate for flex-time, she is greatly interested in knowing how the experiment is working out. That is her primary reason for reading your report. A secondary reason is that she wants data for deciding whether to recommend flex-time for the entire company. Therefore, everything in the report should be directed at those two considerations. Being honest and direct is the most valuable thing you can offer a reader seeking information from you. Even though you know your department head has a real interest in the results of the experiment, you should do nothing to make them look better than they are. If the experiment is a qualified success, and you present it as an unqualified success in order to stroke her ego, then you are doing her a disservice that could potentially undermine her. If, based on your representation of a flawless outcome, she implements flex-time for the entire company and the hidden problems turn out to have disastrous results, then your well-intended deceit might damage her career. So do not be a sycophant who just tells people what they want to hear. Tell them what they need to know: the truth.

On the other hand, your tone should not be cynical or harsh. If the experiment was only a qualified success, you want to be sure to communicate that fact; but you should use language that is tactful. For instance, *The impact on absenteeism was less than expected* is a much more sensitive way of delivering the disappointing news than, *You were wrong about the impact flex-time would have on absenteeism.*

A report directed to your immediate supervisor should generally be detailed, because the supervisor is in a position to understand and act on those details. She will want to know the breakdowns in categories of how many people were present and worked their full shifts under flex-time versus the standard working hours. She will want to know not only whether labor and management liked flex-time, but also which specific groups had specific responses to or problems with the program. You might quote or paraphrase several of the comments you received from workers and their managers. All of these details will give your supervisor a very concrete sense of how the experiment is working out, and that is what she wants to obtain.

If you know that she will use your report to base her decision on whether to extend flex-time to the entire company, you can highlight the main outcomes and other relevant information, even if she did not ask you for them. For instance, if flex-time reduced turn-around-time for requests made to the Technical Support and Duplication departments, because it spread out the same amount of work over more hours, you can point that out, and then add a sentence remarking how certain departments might likewise enjoy this benefit, but not others. Apart from pointing out something she might otherwise overlook, such comments—made in moderation—will make you appear perceptive, self-motivated, and concerned about the performance of your department.

Now, if you were writing the same report for a corporate vice-president based in a different city, how would your writing change?

First, his reason for reading the report would be different from your supervisor's. He is probably interested generally in how the experiment has been proceeding, but he does not care to wade through a lot of details. So, you would write a shorter report that relies more heavily on generalizations. Since all he really wants to know is whether the experiment is working or not, you would announce that right away, probably in the first sentence; certainly in the first paragraph. You might begin the report to the vice-president something like this:

Between October 1 and December 1, the flex-time experiment in the Computer Services Department was a qualified success. It appears to have improved morale and job satisfaction, reduced turn-around time for technical support services, and possibly enhanced productivity slightly. However, employees worked an average of ten minutes a day less, and managers complained that it was sometimes difficult to schedule meetings and coordinate activities when not everyone was working the same hours.

Notice that these opening sentences say everything the vice-president is likely to be interested in knowing. He may even choose to read no further in the report, and be grateful to you for saving his time and attention. He has learned what he needs to know.

Of course, he might still be interested in how you arrived at those conclusions, so you would still need to develop the report. In this case, it would make sense to break down the topic into subsections: **Benefits from Flex-time** and **Problems with Flex-Time.** Then, proceeding one-by-one, discuss each benefit and liability in detail. Notice how, if you use this organizational plan, everything will still point back to the opening paragraph. A well organized report always does that. **That is why the opening paragraph is the most important part of the report.**

Typically, you should write more formally to someone who is several steps ahead of you on the corporate ladder. This does not mean that you should write more awkwardly, use weaker verbs, or invoke more qualifications. But you would not assume the kind of casual rapport you might have with your co-workers or supervisor. You would refer to your colleagues by their titles, avoid office slang, and use precise names for procedures and equipment.

Also, do not assume that high-ranking executives are familiar with the work you do. They may have entirely different backgrounds from yours and may never have done the work of your department. Even if they once did, they certainly are not involved in the detail or state-of-the-art procedures now. So do not take it for granted that they are familiar with the details of your job.

In the flex-time example, the writer must tell the vice-president what he needs to know in order to understand the experiment and its outcomes—

but not more than he needs or wants to know. **This is a critical aspect of all writing, and it involves making the effort to stop and think about how things look from the reader's point of view.**

For instance, if there are three basic corporate approaches to flex-time, Red, White, and Blue, you might remind him of that, explain in a sentence or two the distinguishing features of each, and state briefly which one the experiment employed and why. He does not need to learn the history of flex-time in the United States, however. Notice that you would not bother to explain the Red, White, and Blue plans to your immediate supervisor, because as someone closely involved with the issue, she already knows about them.

Since the vice-president lives out of town, you should always remember that your reader is not familiar with the details of your local operation, the building, or the city. It would be adequate to tell a local reader that using flex-time enables employees to avoid traffic delays on the Palmetto Expressway, because she would be familiar not only with the freeway but also with how the company is situated relative to it. But an out-of-towner needs to be told whether traffic jams on the Palmetto cause major or minor delays. **Remember, you want always to see things from your reader's point of view. If you were he, with his background and level of knowledge about the subject, would these descriptions be adequate?**

Students, too, should think about their reader before writing. For instance, is a book report intended solely for the professor, who has already read the book, or for people who have not? If the former, then you do not need to summarize the book in great depth or repeat a lot of things the professor already knows. Instead, you would comment more on how the book is written, what it achieves, and what it fails to achieve. But if the assignment is to write a review for other students who have never read the book, then you would need to summarize the book's content much more fully and explain its main points in more detail. And you would need to explain terms and concepts that many of your readers may not understand. A report written for a professor would probably analyze and probe more deeply, while one written for people who are unfamiliar with the work under study would provide a greater sense of context, summarize key points, and avoid becoming enmeshed in details or secondary issues that require a lot of explanation.

EXERCISES

1. Identify three people to whom you frequently submit your writing. Make a list of at least three elements that characterize each of them as readers. What kinds of things do they want to find out? What is their level of technical understanding about your work? What is an appropriate tone to use when writing for them? Feel free to add other issues to this list.

2. Write a memo to your immediate supervisor requesting a new piece of equipment that will enable you to perform one of your tasks better.

3. Write a memo requesting the same equipment but addressed to a company vice-president who has a general understanding of what you do, but not a detailed background in your field.

4. Write a memo requesting the same equipment but addressed to the company's budget director, who is trying to reduce expenditures for new equipment throughout the company.

5. Write a memo to a student summer employee who has little experience in your field explaining the function of the new equipment and why you need it.

CHAPTER FOUR
ORGANIZATION
PART I: BUSINESS APPLICATIONS

Identifying your purpose and analyzing your reader are the main ways to make your writing goals clear and explicit. Having an effective organizational plan is the most important strategy for achieving these goals.

In a well organized piece, everything points to some central statement. This statement, often called a **thesis statement**, is the most important link between your goals and what you actually write. One of the greatest writing problems I routinely encounter is that people often do not really know what their writing goals are, or what their real point is, when they start writing. When this happens, the rest of the essay or report tends to be vague and loosely organized. Sometimes people discover their main point as they write. This is fine, **provided that they then go back and modify the thesis statement to express it forthrightly. The more precisely the thesis is articulated, the more focused and penetrating the writing will be.**

The thesis statement should state clearly, directly, and as simply as possible what you want your reader to do or know or believe, and it should indicate the major lines of reasoning or categories of information that comprise the body of the report, memorandum, or analytical study. Often the thesis statement is a single sentence, although sometimes, especially in very long studies, the thesis statement may require two or three sentences. Normally it should be in the first paragraph. In academic writing it typically appears as the final sentence of the first paragraph, but for business writing you can often let it be the opening sentence.

For instance, in Example 1 below, the writer's goal is to convince his supervisor to purchase an iPhone for him. Notice how the initial sentence asserts both the action he want his manager to take and the basic reasons why she should do so. Then the rest of memorandum elaborates on those reasons and concludes by reiterating his request for her to provide him with an iPhone. Also notice how brief the memo is. Effective writing does not need to be lengthy, and it is never convoluted. Readers appreciate it when you make your case directly and then stop. It not only saves them time, it also makes it easier for them to understand what you are saying. Plus, your directness and brevity will make you appear focused and efficient.

EXAMPLE 1
Memorandum Requesting Equipment

TO: Nina Li, Sales Manager
FROM: Bob Hutchinson, Sales Associate
SUBJECT: Request for iPhone
DATE: 11/11/11

****

In order to perform my work more efficiently and remain in contact with you, my co-workers, and clients when I am away from the office, I am requesting an iPhone.

As you know, I am often required to travel for work, both to remote sites locally and to our offices in other cities. Even with a laptop computer, I am often out of contact because I do not have access to a working network. But an iPhone will enable me to remain in touch by voice, email, and text-message, wherever I am.

An iPhone will also enable me to access the online records, client lists, and other information I require for my work. Last week, for instance, I was late in responding to emails from three of our clients because my hotel did not have Internet access. One of those clients has become especially upset about this and is threatening to take her business elsewhere. With an iPhone, I can assure her that this will not happen again. I will also be able to remain in almost constant communication with you and my co-workers in our firm, and this will enable me to respond to your questions and requests in a timely way. The expense to the company will be small compared to the greater efficiency and improved customer satisfaction this purchase will derive. Therefore, I am asking you to approve my request for an iPhone.

The opening sentence is crucial, because it announces the writer's main concern. In Example 1, for instance, the reader could stop reading after the initial sentence and know exactly what the memo is about. Let's assume that the supervisor, Ms. Li, is especially concerned about efficiency and customer relations. The first sentence begins by appealing to both of those concerns. If the author of the memo, Mr. Hutchinson, also knows that Ms. Li believes it is good business to impress clients with the latest technology, he could refer to that in the first sentence as well: *In order to perform my work more efficiently, remain in contact with you, my co-workers and clients when I am away from the office,* **and impress**

***our clients with our company's state-of-the-art technology**, I am requesting an iPhone.* Ultimately, he is advancing his goals but doing it on terms that will resonate with her. That is what strong writing does.

Having stated that an iPhone will make him more efficient and better able to serve his clients, Hutchinson needs to explain more specifically how it will do that. The body of the memo serves this purpose. The second paragraph makes the case that an iPhone will allow him to do things he cannot currently do with just a laptop computer: remain in constant contact through voice, text messaging, and email and have continual access to online resources. **These are the bases for Hutchinson's claim that he will be more efficient with an iPhone. The more precisely such supporting points are stated, the more convincing the argument will be, since it is these details that ground the argument in concrete reality.**

Had Hutchinson simply reiterated that the iPhone will enable him to remain in contact, without specifying how, then he would have shifted the burden of recognizing the exact benefits of an iPhone onto his reader. **It is always a bad practice to expect readers to make critical connections or recognize the details on which generalizations are based, because if they fail to do so, then the point will not be made. *As writers, we must therefore assume responsibility for making everything as explicit as possible, so we will not have to count on our***

readers being able to figure things out for themselves.

The third paragraph of Example 1 argues that an iPhone will enable Hutchinson to achieve greater customer satisfaction, and the reference to his missing communications from three clients allows him to present this argument in a very concrete way. By further elaborating on the angry client who threatened to take her business elsewhere, he both shows the seriousness of the problem and appeals to his supervisor's greatest concern: retaining clients.

PARAGRAPHS AND TOPIC SENTENCES

Notice that the paragraphs in Example 1 are short, and that each develops just one point. In essay and report writing, especially for academic work, paragraphs still focus on one main point, but these typically are broader in scope than the ones in shorter memos. They are also longer—about a quarter to three-quarters of a page is often a good length. This is because essay writing involves developing main points at length, and this normally requires at least three or four sentences, and often more.

But for short business reports and memoranda short paragraphs are often more effective, because they are easier to follow and place less demand on your reader's attention span. And even in essays and longer reports, it is a good idea to break especially long paragraphs into ones that do not exceed three-quarters of page, in order to give your reader a break. Anything that makes your writing easier to read and helps your reader follow your points with minimal effort is an asset. Always let that guide your decisions about how to present your material.

The basic purpose of a paragraph is to assert a main point and then support and elaborate on it. The first sentence, known as the **topic sentence**, does for the paragraph what the thesis statement does for the entire essay. It states the central point precisely and directly and indicates the logic and supporting detail that it depends on.

EXAMPLE 2
Report on the Flex-time Experiment

Paragraph 1
The flex-time experiment in the Computer Services Department was a qualified success. It appears to have improved morale and job satisfaction, reduced turn-around time for technical support services, and possibly enhanced productivity slightly. However, employees worked an average of ten minutes a day less, and managers complained that it was sometimes

difficult to schedule meetings and coordinate activities when not everyone was working the same hours.

Paragraph 2

The experiment appears to have improved morale and job satisfaction by affording employees more choices for how to structure their lives. A survey administered after the three-month trial period showed that 24 of the 32 Computer Services employees who participated felt positively about flex-time (75%). One third of those 24 employees strongly agreed with the statement, "I enjoy my job more with flex-time." The remaining 16 (2/3) agreed, but not strongly. Of the eight employees who did not indicate a positive reaction, four indicated no preference either way, one disagreed with the statement, "I enjoy my job more with flex-time" and three strongly disagreed.

Paragraph 3

The most common reasons for agreeing or strongly agreeing with the statement, "I enjoy my job more with flex-time," were that flex-time enabled employees to structure their schedules to avoid rush hour traffic, coordinate activities with their families, and work according to their own biological rhythms: morning people could come in early and be productive, while evening people could sleep later. (See Appendix 1.)

Paragraph 4

Technical Support was able to serve its clients faster, because it operated for more hours each day. Instead of being open only from 8:30 A.M. until 5:00 P.M., under flex-time technicians were available from 7 A.M. until 6:30 P.M. Consequently, they were able to provide 15% more same-day service than in the previous three-month period. Of the clients who responded to our survey, 21% indicated they were more satisfied with service during the flex-time period than the one preceding it, while the remaining 74% noticed no difference. Five percent were less satisfied. (See Appendix 2.)

Paragraph 5

Overall, productivity within the department rose slightly. Compared to the previous three-month period, when 8 projects were completed on schedule, 2 ahead of schedule and 3 behind schedule, during the flex-time period 10 projects were completed on schedule, 2 ahead of schedule, and 2 behind schedule. And the Technical Support team closed out tickets on 214 clients, up from 194 clients in the previous period—slightly more than a ten percent increase. (See Appendix 3.)

Paragraph 6

On the other hand, some problems with flex-time did occur. The main problem employees identified was that they were sometimes frustrated at not being able to consult with co-workers when problems arose. Instead of having access to all of their co-workers for 8 hours each day, morning and evening workers often overlapped for only 5 or 6 hours, and this sometimes caused delays. Even those with overall positive responses to flex-time acknowledged they sometimes experienced difficulties coordinating with co-workers, but only 3 of the 32 employees agreed that this was a serious problem, while 2 others called it a significant problem. The remaining 27 employees indicated that the problems coordinating with co-workers were either minimal or none.

Paragraph 7

Managers, however, were significantly less enthusiastic about flex-time than employees. Tardiness was up 18% compared to the previous three-month period, and several managers complained that it was difficult to schedule meetings when everyone could attend and that it was sometimes difficult to contact employees when unexpected difficulties arose. Overall, only 22% of managers strongly agreed or agreed that flex-time represents an improvement over the regular schedule, while 28% strongly agreed and 36% agreed that the regular schedule was superior. The remaining 14% were neutral. (See Appendix 4.)

Paragraph 8

In conclusion, the results of the flex-time experiment were mixed. Employees greatly preferred having a flex-time option, and their morale and productivity improved significantly with it. Overall, clients were also slightly more satisfied with the service they received during the flex-time experiment than during the previous three-month period; however, the majority did not notice a significant difference. Managers, on the other hand, found that flex-time complicated their work, making it difficult to schedule meetings and coordinate activities among workers. In contrast to their subordinates, managers preferred their regular, fixed schedule by a ratio of three to one.

Appendix 1

This appendix would include the statistics, employees' responses, managers' responses, and other raw data pertaining to employee morale and job satisfaction.

Appendix 2

This appendix would include the statistics, user responses, and other raw data pertaining to how well Tech Support performed.

Appendix 3

This appendix would include the statistics and other raw data pertaining to productivity.

Appendix 4

This appendix would include the statistics, managers' responses, and other raw data pertaining to managers' responses to flex-time.

Note the structure of each of the paragraphs in this report. The job of the first paragraph is to present the overall conclusion and to indicate the main line of reasoning behind it. While in academic writing the thesis statement usually appears as the final sentence in the first paragraph, in this sort of business report, whose reader does not require an explanation of the flex-time experiment and how and why it was conducted, there is no reason not to present the main conclusion in the first sentence: *The flex-time experiment. . .was a qualified success.* The rest of the paragraph sets up the body of the essay by presenting each of the supporting points on which this conclusion rests.

The first supporting point for this thesis initially appears in the second sentence of Paragraph 1: *The experiment appears to have improved morale and job satisfaction.* Notice how the entire second paragraph is devoted to developing that point. Indeed, Paragraph 2 begins with a topic statement that both reiterates and elaborates upon it: *The experiment appears to have improved morale and job satisfaction by affording employees more choices for how to structure their lives.*

Good topic sentences do this. By reiterating a main point in the thesis statement they connect their paragraph to the thesis statement—thereby maintaining a tight focus on the report's central conclusion and showing the relevance of the paragraph to the central argument. At the same time, they elaborate on the thesis statement, thereby taking the discussion of a specific main point to a deeper, more concrete level.

In Paragraph 2, for instance, the first part of the topic sentence reiterates that flex-time improved morale and job satisfaction, while the second part elaborates by stating how it achieves this goal: by affording employees more choices for how to structure their lives. Everything else that follows in the Paragraphs 2 and 3 somehow shows that flex-time improved morale and job satisfaction by giving employees more control over the structure of their lives.

Because the factual support here is based on statistical analysis of a survey, the writer has chosen also to present the raw data in a chart in Appendix 1. Placing an optional table or chart in an appendix allows interested readers to view the data without impeding the flow of the discussion. On the other hand, if the writer deems that it is important for readers to see the raw data in numerical form as they are reading, he or she can incorporate a chart, table, or graph directly into the text, following the narrative discussion.

The next main point asserted in the second sentence of Paragraph 1 is that flex-time reduced turn-around time for Technical Support Services. Notice how this point also serves as the topic sentence for Paragraph 4: *Technical Support was able to serve its clients faster, because it operated for more hours each day.* This topic sentence not only reiterates the main point from the thesis in the first paragraph, it also refines that point by stating why flex-time improved efficiency: *because it operated for more hours each day.* The remainder of the paragraph provides the factual details that support this conclusion.

Notice that each of the remaining paragraphs centers on one of the main points presented in the first paragraph and then supports and elaborates upon it. This practice gives the report a very clear structure that makes it easy for readers to follow, even though it contains a lot of factual and statistical data.

Also notice that individual facts and statistics always appear *after* the point they support, *not before*. This practice creates a context for understanding the relevance or significance of the factual and statistical details, so the readers understand immediately why you are telling them these things. If you present the details first, then readers will have to wait until they come to the conclusion in order to know why you are telling this. Unlike in story writing, where the purpose is to create drama and suspense, report writing strives to present factual information in a clear, organized fashion, and it seeks to achieve no dramatic effects. Therefore, it is best to assert conclusions and main points at the beginning. In other words, **always state the bottom line first.**

OUTLINE OF EXAMPLE 2
The flex-time experiment was a qualified success.

I. Flex-time improved morale, reduced turn-around time for Tech Support, and improved productivity.

    A. Flex-time improved morale and job satisfaction by giving employees greater choice in how to structure their lives.

        1. Summary of statistics supporting this conclusion

        2. Ways that flex-time gave employees greater choice

            a. Able to avoid rush hour traffic

            b. Able to coordinate activities with families

            c. Able to work according to their own biological rhythms

    B. Flex-time reduced turn-around time for Tech Support and produced somewhat greater customer satisfaction.

        1. Able to keep longer hours

            a. Open 7:00 AM to 6:30 PM

        2. Somewhat greater customer satisfaction

            a. Statistics supporting this conclusion

    C. Flex-time slightly improved productivity

        1. More projects were completed on time

            a. Statistics supporting this conclusion

        2. Tech Support closed more tickets

          a. Statistics supporting this conclusion
II. Qualifications to flex-time's success
    A. Employees were frustrated by delays caused by not being able to contact co-workers.
        1. Statistics supporting this conclusion
    B. Managers prefer regular schedule
        1. Statistics supporting this conclusion
        2. Reasons given by managers
            a. Hard to schedule meetings
            b. Hard to contact employees at all times
    C. Tardiness increased
        1. Statistics supporting this conclusion

MORE ON TOPIC SENTENCES

Topic sentences are the real workhorses of strong essays. Effective topic sentences always both point back to some aspect of the thesis statement and indicate how the paragraph will elaborate on it. And the more focused and precise the topic sentence is, the deeper and more incisive the analysis in the body of the paragraph can be. *More than anything else, formulating precise thesis statements and topic sentences is the key to writing incisive, well developed, effectively structured reports and essays.*

It may at first seem incongruous, but expanding on the topic sentence actually involves narrowing the focus and becoming increasingly specific, not more generalized and vague. **Paragraph construction should move from the general to the specific.** The topic sentence should be more specific than the thesis statement, and the body of each supporting paragraph should be more specific and more concrete than the topic sentence. For instance, in Example 2, the facts and statistics in the body of the paragraphs are more specific and concrete than the topic sentences. *One third of those 24 employees, strongly agreed with the statement, "I enjoy my job more with flex-time,"* is more specific than the topic sentence: *The experiment appears to have improved morale and job satisfaction.* And, *The Technical Support team closed out tickets on 214 clients, up from 194 clients in the previous period*, is more concrete than the topic sentence: *Overall, productivity within the department rose slightly.* The statistics and quotes from the survey are the basic facts on which such conclusions as flex-time improved employee morale and slightly increased productivity are based. To make any conclusion compelling, you must strive to root it in concrete reality. But state the conclusion first as a topic sentence, because this provides the context through which the reader considers the facts and figures; it makes the details relevant.

In summary, organization and development are the bases of rigorous argument. A sound organization will allow you to explore a topic more deeply, in a more probing fashion, because its general-to-specific development pushes you to become increasingly precise. Essays structured around strong thesis statements and topic sentences that clearly assert main points and supporting conclusions will permit deeper exploration than essays structured around vague, imprecise, or less focused statements. When you are writing, and especially when you proofread, you should be aware of your thesis statement and topic sentences, and you should repeatedly challenge yourself to see that they express your meaning as accurately, clearly, and concretely as possible. Always feel free to revise, refine and sharpen the focus of these crucial statements as you work through the drafts of the essay.

ADDITIONAL SAMPLE THESIS AND TOPIC SENTENCES

1. Strong thesis: By lowering interest rates and lowering taxes the government hopes to stimulate the economy.

    Strong supporting topic sentence: The government hopes that lowering interest rates will stimulate the economy by giving more people and companies access to affordable money and by discouraging savings.

    Strong supporting topic sentence: The government hopes that lowering taxes will free-up money for investment in new business ventures, inventories, expansion, and equipment upgrades. It also hopes that lowering taxes will encourage companies and individuals to produce higher earnings.

[Notice how this thesis and its supporting topic sentences highlight the logical relationships by using phrases beginning *By*.... The *by* phrases tell us how things will happen. Notice that they push the discussion deeper, to a more specific level. Lowering interest rates and taxes is a more concrete concept than stimulating the economy. *Because* phrases do the same thing for cause-effect relationships.]

Mediocre thesis: For various reasons the government wants to lower interest rates and taxes.

Mediocre supporting topic sentence: The government hopes that lowering interest rates will stimulate the economy.

Mediocre supporting topic sentence: The government hopes that lowering taxes will stimulate the economy.

[Notice how the strong thesis statement develops the topic more sharply. The strong thesis incorporates everything found in the thesis statement and topic sentences from this mediocre example, but because the strong thesis statement is more precise and more efficient, the topic sentences that amplify upon it can also develop their points more precisely, at a more concrete level. Therefore, the essay built around the strong thesis statement will probably discuss the topic more specifically, in greater depth, and more efficiently.]

Weak thesis: A connection exists among interest rates, taxes, and the economy.

   Weak supporting topic sentence: There is a connection between interest rates and the economy.

   [Notice how vague this is in comparison to the strong thesis.]

Very weak thesis: In this paper I will discuss interest rates, taxes, and the economy.

   [Notice how this thesis neither presents a conclusion nor asserts a main point.]

   Very weak supporting topic sentence: The prime rate is what banks charge their most favored customers.

   [Notice how this sentence neither points back to the thesis nor asserts a main point for the paragraph to develop.]

2. Strong thesis: If we reinforce the foundation with pilings and add a series of windbreaks on the ocean side, the structure will be able to withstand a Category 5 hurricane.

   Strong topic sentence: Reinforced concrete pilings will ensure structural integrity by protecting against erosion.

   Strong topic sentence: Windbreaks on the ocean shore will diminish the intensity of wind gusts that might damage the structure. [Notice how specific the thesis and topic sentences are. Note especially how the topic sentences do more than introduce the idea that the pilings and windbreaks will reinforce the structure; they specify exactly how they will reinforce it.]

Mediocre thesis: Pilings and windbreaks will strengthen the structure against a hurricane.
    Mediocre topic sentence: Hurricane tides can cause erosion.
    Mediocre topic sentence: Category 5 hurricane winds exceed 140 miles per hour.
    [Notice that the thesis is less specific than the strong thesis. Also, although the mediocre topic sentences introduce relevant considerations—erosion and the hurricane winds—they do not mention either the pilings or windbreaks.]

Weak thesis: We can strengthen the structure to withstand hurricanes.
    Weak topic sentence: We need to protect the structure from erosion and the high winds.
    [Notice how the strong thesis statement is more specific than even the weak topic sentence. Here neither the weak thesis nor weak topic sentence even mentions what will strengthen the structure: pilings and windbreaks.]

3. Strong thesis: The introduction of the horse to the Great Plains Indians of North America enabled them to hunt more successfully and travel greater distances.

Strong topic sentence: The horse enabled the Great Plains Indians to hunt new species of game, especially the buffalo, and to search for game over wider areas.

Strong topic sentence: As a pack animal and a vehicle for transportation, the horse also enabled entire tribes to travel great distances.

Mediocre thesis: The introduction of the horse to the Great Plains Indians of North America changed their lives in several important ways.

Mediocre topic sentence: One way the horse changed their lives was to make them better hunters.

Mediocre topic sentence: Horses also made it possible for tribes to travel farther.

Weak thesis: The introduction of the horse was important to the Great Plains Indians of North America.

Weak topic sentence: The horse changed their lives.

CHAPTER FIVE
ORGANIZATION
PART II: ACADEMIC ESSAYS

The same basic principles apply both to business and academic writing. However, academic writing is often more analytical, and this presents some special challenges. When writing academic papers whose purpose is to analyze, rely upon a strong thesis statement to assert the main points and their logical relationship to each other; then develop each point within a paragraph or related group of paragraphs that centers around a specific topic sentence that refines it even further.

While not everyone likes to work from outlines as highly detailed as the one at the end of this chapter, it is a good idea at least to sketch out the main conclusions and the flow of logic among your main points before you begin writing the full essay. Personally, I often use the first paragraph, especially the thesis statement, to figure out the essay's overall direction, and then I refer back to it as I write, much as someone else might refer back to an outline. Use whatever approach you find most comfortable, and do not get caught up in the formal rules for formatting outlines or organizational hierarchies. But as your first step in writing, develop a strong sense of where you are going in the essay and how you plan to get there. Your ultimate purpose in writing should determine the direction your essay takes.

Let's look at the structure of the sample essay below, an analysis of the evolution of Shakespeare's tragic heroes. Even if you are unfamiliar with the plays *Romeo and Juliet*, *Julius Caesar*, and/or *Hamlet*, or if you disagree with the essay's conclusions, you can nonetheless observe how the thesis statement and topic sentences provide an organizational structure that both unifies the essay and encourages development of the main points. At the end of the discussion are an outline and hierarchical chart to help you examine the structure more readily.

ACADEMIC WRITING EXAMPLE

Paragraph 1

Shakespeare's tragic heroes in Romeo and Juliet, Julius Caesar, *and* Hamlet, *evolve from a protagonist who has **restricted freedom of choice** in his actions and no real moment of **tragic recognition** to protagonists who have complete freedom and achieve **recognition**. Romeo's **responsibility for his fate** is relatively limited, whereas Brutus and Hamlet determine their own outcomes to considerably greater degrees. This higher level of **responsibility** and **insight** makes Brutus and Hamlet **more fully tragic figures**. Because Hamlet achieves the greatest level of **insight**, he is the most **tragic** of the three protagonists.*

Paragraph 2

*Romeo's **responsibility for his fate** and his capacity for **tragic recognition** are limited because Romeo has little control over the no-win circumstances that determine his life. Romeo's **freedom of choice is restricted** to the possibilities others introduce, and, for the most part, Romeo must respond to situations that spring up around him. Except for marrying Juliet, he does not create the situations in which he finds himself. For instance, he can attend or not attend Old Capulet's party; he can fight or not fight Tybalt; he can accept or refuse his banishment, but these choices are all thrust upon him. Even his suicide comes about in response* *to a situation he did not create--Juliet's apparent death. Significantly, only when Romeo and Juliet marry do they exceed the limits imposed upon them and act to create their destinies.*

Paragraph 3

Moreover, apart from his decision to crash the party, a decision that hardly merits the death penalty, Romeo always confronts no-win decisions. He can turn-in Tybalt to the Prince, thereby appeasing the social authority but denying his friendship to Mercutio, whom Tybalt has killed; or he can act like a loyal friend, avenge Mercutio by fighting Tybalt, and undermine the social order. He can accept banishment and remain apart from Juliet, or return and risk death. He can commit suicide, a deadly sin, or accept an empty life without Juliet--until the Prince executes him for Paris' death.

Paragraph 4

Because Romeo's demise stems primarily from situations he did not initiate and could not control, we cannot say that he falls from fortune because of a tragic flaw. Consequently, there can be no moment of ***tragic recognition****, for there is nothing for Romeo to recognize: his fate did not emanate from a personality defect. True, Romeo's youth, passion and rashness help bring him down, but they are less central to his demise than the impossible circumstances he finds himself in. A star-crossed lover, indeed, Romeo is ultimately more unfortunate than tragic.*

Paragraph 5

Brutus in Julius Caesar, *on the other hand, is far more responsible for his fate because he **possesses greater freedom of choice**; however his tragic stature is diminished because he fails to adequately **recognize** his flaw. As with the Aristotelian tragic hero, excessive pride undermines Brutus by provoking him to exercise his **freedom of choice** unwisely. He is completely free to reject Cassius's offer to join the conspiracy; indeed, he has the power to foil the coup entirely. However, Cassius appeals successfully to Brutus' pride to persuade him to lead the conspiracy, thereby initiating Brutus' doom. Later, pride in his oratory skills blinds Brutus to the danger of allowing Antony to speak at Caesar's funeral; then pride in his military prowess leads Brutus to insist that his own army fight on a disadvantageous battlefield. Most importantly, Brutus' pride leads him to believe he should elevate his own judgment about Caesar's danger to Rome over the judgment of the Senate and people of the Roman Republic.*

Paragraph 6

Because Julius Caesar *enacts the fall of an essentially good and powerful man due to excessive pride, it represents something very akin to classical Greek tragedy. But Brutus **never completely recognizes** how his pride has brought him down; admitting that he "owe[s] more tears" to Caesar is not enough (V,v,101). Consequently, Brutus' **tragic stature is diminished**, but* *not altogether obliterated.*

Paragraph 7

*On the other hand, by **recognizing** his fundamental identity, Hamlet ultimately **accepts responsibility for his actions** and **gains insight** into himself, his situation and his actions. Initially events confuse Hamlet who, like Romeo, must react to circumstances he did not create. Like Brutus, Hamlet enjoys considerable **freedom of action**, and in his confusion he creates many of the subsequent circumstances that accumulate to destroy him. However, once he **achieves clarity** about his role as the proper heir to the throne of Denmark, Hamlet overcomes despair, restores order in the kingdom and **achieves full tragic stature.***

Paragraph 8

*Hamlet achieves his **identity** by learning the proper priorities to guide his actions and choices. He is simultaneously a son, a prince, an avenger and a lover, and he responds in each of these capacities to the news of his father's murder and his mother's remarriage to his uncle Claudius, who, Hamlet learns from his father's ghost, killed his father, the king of Denmark. When the demands of being an avenger conflict with those of being a lover, son or prince, Hamlet becomes confused, despairing and indecisive; he acts inconsistently and loses opportunities to set things right. His failure to know the proper priorities among his roles ultimately sows the seeds of his destruction. When he forgoes killing Claudius at* *prayer because to do so would send Claudius to Heaven instead of Hell, Hamlet wrongly allows his role of avenger to supersede his role as heir to the throne, whose paramount duty is to liberate Denmark from Claudius, the usurper. Because he misplaces his priorities Hamlet loses his only chance to eliminate Claudius without incurring his own death.*

Paragraph 9

*Only when Hamlet **recognizes** that his most important identity is as heir to the throne and that his first obligation is to ensure Denmark's well being does he overcome his indecisiveness and despair. Upon his return to Denmark in Act V he proclaims himself Hamlet, "the Dane," (V,i, 258) an epithet reserved for the king. His final act, naming Fortinbras as his successor, underscores his identification with his kingly role. Thus, he has **recognized** and rectified his earlier shortcoming in self-knowledge. He knows how he must act; he accepts that he must kill Claudius. He is wiser, more fulfilled and more at peace with himself when he enters the fencing match than he was in Act I. By the final act Hamlet has gained the self-knowledge requisite for **full tragic stature.***

ANALYSIS OF THE SAMPLE ESSAY

Let's analyze this essay in terms of its purpose, readership and organization and development. First, what is the purpose of the essay? The thesis statement normally announces the purpose. Here, the last two sentences of the first paragraph state the paper's main conclusion: that Brutus and Hamlet are more fully tragic than Romeo because they are more responsible for their own fates and they achieve greater insight into their actions. Hamlet is the most fully tragic because he achieves the greatest insight. The essay's purpose, then, is to demonstrate this conclusion as clearly as possible by showing the exact nature of each character's level of responsibility and insight. In academic writing the purpose of the essay is usually to proclaim and explain some meaningful conclusion. **The more precisely you present your conclusion in the thesis statement, the more focused you will remain on achieving your basic purpose.**

Notice that even though the thesis in the sample is fairly broad—it encompasses judgments about three separate literary characters— it is also quite specific. Had I substituted a less specific thesis my purpose would have become vague. For example, I might I have stated that *Romeo, Brutus, and Hamlet each achieve different levels of responsibility and insight.* Such a statement would still have structured the essay, inviting distinct sections describing each character's level of responsibility for his fate and insight into his actions. But it would not have asserted the terms in which these protagonists are different, nor would it have stated the main conclusion about the comparison: that these differences make Hamlet and Brutus more fully tragic. Thus the original thesis, which says much more about the characters than that they are simply "different," better succeeds in achieving my purpose, which is to present my main conclusions as completely and precisely as possible.

Usually the reader of a college student's essay is the course professor. I suggest that most professors want two things. First, they look for a serious, rigorous, carefully reasoned, well focused, thoughtful discussion of the subject. This is true for any academic reader, regardless of the academic discipline. Second, because they must evaluate their students' achievements, professors look for evidence that students understand the issues under discussion and have taken into account any relevant considerations that they should reasonably be expected to know about. In the case of this essay, I assumed that my reader, a college professor, knew Shakespeare had written the plays and was familiar with them. So I did not have to begin by summarizing the plots or telling her the plays were by Shakespeare. Instead I was able to begin with a strong assertion about how Shakespeare's tragic figures evolve and then build to my thesis statement.

I also assumed that my reader was familiar with discussions about tragedy and so did not need me to explain basic concepts, such as the relationship between a tragic hero's level of insight about himself and his tragic stature. I knew that she was mostly interested in how I would distinguish among these three Shakespearean protagonists and that the more precisely I could express what separates Romeo from Brutus, and Brutus from Hamlet, in terms of their tragic stature, the more satisfied my reader would be.

I therefore chose an organizational structure that allows me to explore each character very systematically, specifically in terms of their responsibility for their fates and their levels of insight. We can see that the main thesis rests upon other conclusions I must draw about each character. In a very basic way we can view this entire essay as a main conclusion supported by a systematic hierarchy of supporting conclusions.

The top level of the hierarchy is, of course, the thesis statement: **This higher level of responsibility and insight makes Brutus and Hamlet more fully tragic figures. Because Hamlet achieves the greatest level of insight, he is the most tragic of the three protagonists.** (Paragraph 1). This main conclusion results from the supporting conclusions presented in the topic sentences for each section: *Romeo's responsibility for his fate and his capacity for tragic recognition are limited because Romeo has little control over the no-win circumstances that determine his life (Paragraph 2); Brutus. . .is far more responsible for his fate because he possesses greater freedom of choice; however his tragic stature is diminished because he fails to adequately recognize his flaw (Paragraph*

5); and . . . *by recognizing his fundamental identity Hamlet ultimately accepts responsibility for his actions and gains insight into himself, his situation and his actions* (Paragraph 7). Notice how each of these topic sentences points back directly to the thesis statement; each topic sentence talks about a character's level of responsibility for his fate and his level of recognition. Moreover, each topic sentence does more than simply reiterate its part of the thesis; it makes a strong assertion about the particular nature of each character's responsibility and insight.

Thus, for example, *Romeo's responsibility for his fate and his capacity for tragic recognition are limited because Romeo has little control over the no-win circumstances that determine his life*, both points back to the first paragraph, which states that he has restricted freedom of choice, and expands upon it by describing the nature of the restriction—his possibilities are introduced by others and he finds himself in no-win situations. This exemplifies how a topic sentence lends focus and unity to the essay by linking the paragraph to the overall thesis, as it amplifies a main point by making it more specific. **Remember, more than anything else, formulating precise thesis statements and topic sentences is the key to writing incisive, well developed, effectively structured reports and essays.**

Paragraph construction should move from the general to the specific. The topic sentence should be more specific than the thesis statement, and the body of each supporting paragraph should be more specific and more concrete than the topic sentence. For example, the topic sentence in Paragraph 5 states, *Brutus. . .is far more responsible for his fate because he possesses greater freedom of choice.* This sentence amplifies on the thesis statement, which says that Brutus is more responsible than Romeo but does not state why. Likewise, the body of Paragraph 5 becomes more precise than the topic sentence. The body points out how excessive pride induces Brutus to exercise his freedom of choice unwisely, and then it becomes more specific still, identifying particular instances where Brutus' pride harms him by causing him to make poor choices.

Sentences that show logical relationships make very strong topic sentences. For example, consider the topic sentence in Paragraph 4: *Because Romeo's demise stems primarily from situations he did not initiate and could not control, we cannot say that he falls because of a tragic flaw.* Here I use *because* to indicate the cause-effect relationship between Romeo's lack of control and his failure to qualify for tragic stature. By beginning with a topic sentence that asserts a logical relationship I sharpen the focus of the discussion.[1]

---

[1] Disregard the "rule," which does not exist, that says you cannot begin a sentence with *because.* Beginning with *because* or any other subordinator will create a dependent clause that must be fused to an independent clause to create a complete sentence. But if you

One of the main sentences in Paragraph 5 likewise shows a logical relationship: *. . .excessive pride undermines Brutus **by** provoking him to exercise his freedom of choice unwisely.* Notice that the sentence not only states that Brutus' pride undermines him, it also specifies **how** this happens: pride provokes him to act unwisely. The rest of the paragraph then develops that narrowly defined topic, identifying the particular instances where Brutus' pride leads him to make unwise, harmful decisions. **By emphasizing the logical relationship between responsibility and freedom of choice, the sentence gives a sharper, more probing edge to the analysis.**

Paragraph 7 demonstrates how to develop a subtopic more fully. It introduces the *Hamlet* section by uniting it with the thesis statement, asserting that Hamlet achieves full tragic stature. The paragraph also serves as a topic sentence for the entire section. The second sentence introduces the idea that Hamlet becomes confused because he must react to circumstances out of his control, and Paragraph 8 expands on that point. The third sentence in Paragraph 7 discusses Hamlet's freedom of action and how his confusion causes him to create the circumstances that destroy him. Paragraph 8 elaborates on that point also. Paragraph 9 expands on the conclusion reached in the final sentence of Paragraph 7: once Hamlet recognizes his proper identity he

---

do fuse it to an independent clause, there is no problem. (See Chapter 6.) In this case the independent clause is: *we cannot say that he falls because of a tragic flaw.*

overcomes despair, restores the kingdom, and achieves tragic stature.

Thus, the section on Hamlet really functions as a "mini-essay" within the larger essay. It develops a distinct thesis that could stand alone if it had to. However, the topic sentence in Paragraph 7 also integrates the Hamlet mini-essay within the larger thesis of the paper. In terms of the mini-essay, Paragraph 7 can also stand alone, or it can serve as an introductory paragraph that establishes the structure for elaborating on the main points of the mini-essay.

I have placed some words and phrases in bold face print to demonstrate how the repetition of key words and concepts from the thesis statement can unify the essay. Repeating *recognition*, *insight*, and *responsibility* within the body of supporting paragraphs induces the reader to associate those paragraphs with the thesis. The deliberate repetition of key words also compels the writer to remain tightly focused on the thesis.

OUTLINE OF THE SAMPLE ESSAY

Thesis: Their higher level of responsibility and insight makes Brutus and Hamlet more fully tragic figures than Romeo. Because Hamlet achieves the greatest level of insight, he is the most tragic of the three protagonists.

I. "Romeo's responsibility for his fate and his capacity for tragic recognition are limited because Romeo has little control over the no-win circumstances that determine his life." [Topic sentence for Paragraph 2]

    A. "Romeo's freedom of choice is restricted to the possibilities others introduce."

        1. He did not create his circumstances.

            a. Old Capulet's Party

            b. Fight with Tybalt

            c. Banishment

            d. Juliet's apparent death

        2. He did choose to marry Juliet.

    B. Romeo always confronts no-win situations.

        1. Fight Tybalt or turn him in

        2. Accept banishment or risk death

        3. Commit suicide or live without Juliet

        4. Conclusion that circumstances are more responsible than character flaws for Romeo's demise; he is therefore more unfortunate than tragic.

    C. "Because Romeo's demise stems primarily from situations he did not initiate and could not control, we cannot say that he falls because of a tragic flaw. Consequently, there can be no moment of tragic recognition." [Topic sentence for Paragraph 4]

II. "Brutus, on the other hand, is far more responsible for his fate because he possesses greater freedom of choice; however his tragic stature is diminished because he fails to adequately recognize his flaw." [Topic Sentence for Paragraph 5]

    A. Pride provokes him to exercise his freedom of choice unwisely, thereby creating the circumstances of his downfall.

        1. Cassius plays on Brutus' pride to persuade him to join the conspiracy.

        2. Brutus' pride in his oratory skills blinds him to the danger of allowing Antony to speak at Caesar's funeral.

        3. Brutus' pride leads him to accept a battlefield that places him at a disadvantage.

        4. Brutus' pride elevates his judgment over that of the citizens and Senate of the Republic.

    B. Brutus' tragic stature is diminished because he never recognizes how pride has brought him down.

        1. Owing Caesar more tears is insufficient .

III. By recognizing his fundamental identity Hamlet ultimately accepts responsibility for his actions and gains insight into himself, his situation, and his actions. [Topic sentence for Paragraph 7]

    A. Hamlet achieves his identity by learning the proper priorities to guide his actions. [Topic sentence for Paragraph 8]

1. Hamlet has several identities: son, lover, avenger, prince.
2. When demands of identities conflict, Hamlet becomes confused and indecisive.
    a. He sows the seeds of his destruction by elevating his avenger role over his princely role when he fails to kill Claudius at prayer.

B. In recognizing his proper identity Hamlet overcomes his indecisiveness and gains full tragic stature.
1. He recognizes his most important role is heir to the throne.
    a. He returns as Hamlet, "The Dane."
    b. He names Fortinbras as his successor.
2. The recognition elevates him to full tragic stature.

CHAPTER 6
GRAMMAR

Contrary to popular belief, grammar has a more basic function than being a tool of oppression by English teachers. Writing is foremost a mechanism for communication. Whereas speech involves personal interaction as well as language, writing relies exclusively on language to communicate. Thus, when I say, *Give the forms to her*, I can avoid confusion by pointing to the particular woman I mean. I can also use pauses, facial expressions, vocal intonations, and other non-verbal gestures to facilitate my communication and make my meanings clear. In writing, however, none of those mechanisms is available to help me clarify my meaning and avoid ambiguities. At the level of individual sentences, that function is performed by grammar.

Grammar is essentially a convention by which all users of a language agree that certain practices will mean specific things. If the writer and the readers both know and subscribe to this convention, then their communication will be more precise. And that is why mastery of at least the fundamentals of grammar is important. However, an alarming number of high school graduates, college graduates, and professionals are not fluent in these conventions, probably because they had unpleasant experiences learning them in elementary or middle school. Learning grammar, however, is no more difficult than learning the procedures required for most other tasks we perform daily at the office or in school. So, if you feel you are particularly weak in grammar, I recommend that you buy a basic grammar book and spend a few hours going through it. You will be surprised at how much you can master in just an hour or two, because grammar is actually not difficult. Try to grasp the rationale behind the rules. That way you can figure out what you should do, even if you forget a particular rule.

For those who cannot review a grammar textbook, I will here discuss the fundamentals of English grammar and some of the most common mistakes. These usually stem from the writer's failure to think in terms of sentences, which are comprised of nouns and verbs and other parts of speech.

THE MAJOR PARTS OF SPEECH:
VERBS, NOUNS, PRONOUNS, ADJECTIVES, ADVERBS

In physics we think in terms of matter and energy. Nouns correspond to matter and verbs to energy. Verbs like *read*, *write*, *speak*, *compute*, *calculate*, *analyze*, *multiply*, and *investigate* do not allude to physical things or concepts; they invoke action.

Verbs are the most important part of speech. They infuse the sentence with energy; they animate the static nouns and, in a sense, bring them to life. Strong writing therefore employs forceful, assertive, active verbs. As much as possible, place the weight of the meaning on verbs instead of nouns. For instance, in the sentence, *Brian is the manager of the store*, what are the most important words? They are *Brian*, the subject of the sentence, and *manager*, a noun that conveys most of the sentence's meaning. The verb is *is,* one of the so-called verbs of being. The other verbs of being are *am*, *are*, *was*, *were*, and *will be*. These are the weakest verbs possible because they do not indicate any action or energy, just static existence.

However, if I rewrite the sentence as, *Brian manages the store*, the word that carries the weight of the meaning is now an active verb, *manages*. Say both sentences aloud. Notice how much more direct, compact, and forceful the second one is. This is because a verb, not a noun, conveys the essential meaning. The revised sentence uses fewer words and projects energy. **Placing the weight of your meaning on active verbs instead of nouns will do more to strengthen your writing style than anything else.**

Nouns, on the other hand, are the names of people, places, and things. Typically they have a physical existence—*ball*, *dog*, *computer*, *airplane*—but sometimes they are more abstract, conceptual, or intangible than matter. Even then nouns exist as *things*: thoughts, emotions, plans, institutions, principles, ideas, etc. For instance, *university*, *corporation*, *government*, *conservatism*, *capitalism*, *anger*, *love*, *estimates*, and *truth* are all nouns, even though they do not have physical existence. Proper nouns are the names of people, places, and institutions, and their first letter is capitalized: *Jim*, *Isabel*, *Romania*, and *Congress* are proper nouns.

Pronouns are words that refer back to and replace specific nouns. The singular pronouns in English are *I*, *you*, *he*, *she*, and *it*, when they are in the so-called subjective (or nominative) case—in other words, when they act as the subject of the sentence. (See below.) The plural pronoun in the subjective case is always *they*, regardless of whether it refers to males, females, or inanimate things. Otherwise, we use the so-called objective or possessive cases of pronouns. Broadly speaking, we use the objective case when the pronoun is receiving the action of the sentence rather than performing it. The objective case singular pronouns are *me*, *you*, *him*, *her*, and *it*; the objective case plural pronoun is *them*. Or, if we want to show that a pronoun possesses something, we use the possessive case: *my* book, *your* car, *his* speech, *her* trophy, and *its* charm. The plural possessive case pronoun is always *their*.

Nouns are modified or embellished by adjectives—words that describe them: *deep* thoughts, *ridiculous* plans, *bright* ideas. Verbs are modified by adverbs—words that describe how they act: read *carefully*, write *quickly*, speak *erroneously*, compute *accurately*, investigate *completely*, etc. Often adverbs will end in *ly*, but not always i.e. run *fast*, hit *hard*, paint *well*, etc. Words that end in *ly* will almost always be adverbs; the others can also serve as adjectives, depending on whether they modify verbs or nouns. For example *fast* serves as an adjective in *fast car* but as an adverb in, *The car runs fast.*

WHAT IS A SENTENCE?

A sentence always pairs a subject and verb. Subjects are always nouns or pronouns, and they link with verbs to form a complete unit of thought. Subjects are the matter upon which the energy of the verbs acts. (In rare cases the subject may be implied instead of actually written. For instance, *Go to the store* is a complete sentence that implies the pronoun *You* is the subject of the verb *go*: [*You*] *go to the store*.) The subject and verb must agree with each other in every respect. Not only should a singular verb form accompany a singular subject and a plural verb form join with a plural subject, but it must make sense conceptually to pair the two together.

CLAUSES

Units of subject and verbs are called clauses. All complete sentences are comprised of at least one clause and often only one clause. But not all clauses are complete sentences. As their name suggests, **independent clauses** can stand freely, by themselves, as complete sentences: *I returned home.* **Dependent clauses**, also called **subordinate clauses,** cannot stand alone by themselves; they **depend** upon their connection to an independent clause in order to form a complete sentence, such as, **Because I lost my wallet**, *I returned home. I lost my wallet* makes sense by itself and can stand alone as a complete sentence. But *Because I lost my wallet* makes no sense by itself; it must be joined to the independent clause, *I returned home.*

Both dependent and independent clauses contain a subject and verb. However, placing certain words, called subordinators, at the beginning of independent clauses transforms them into dependent clauses. Consider the example, *After the value of my stock portfolio rose, I bought a boat.* Notice how I created a new, grammatically correct sentence by affixing the independent clause, *I bought a boat*, to the dependent clause, *After the value of my stock portfolio rose.* Also notice that the order between the dependent and independent clauses does not matter. I could just as properly have written, *I bought a boat after the value of my stock portfolio rose.* But I could not simply write, *After the value of my stock portfolio rose.* **We merge dependent and independent clauses to show logical relationships.** In the example above, *after* shows time sequence. It also implies a cause-effect relationship: the increase in value was the cause of my purchasing the boat. *Since* can also show both time sequence and causation: *Since I received my promotion, my free time has evaporated.*

Because indicates cause-effect relationships more explicitly: *Because I received a good tip, I invested in renewable energy.* *Although* indicates a contradiction of what a person might normally expect: *Although the NASDAQ fell by 50 points, I made a killing anyway.* Logically, a 50 point drop in the stock market would lead us to expect a loss, but here that expectation is contradicted. *If* also shows the dependency of one set of conditions on another: *If it does not rain, I will play tennis tonight.*

When, *after*, *since*, *because*, *although*, and *if* are the most common subordinators, so keep an eye out for them when you proofread. Using dependent clauses like these to indicate logical relationships yields strong and effective writing. But you must be sure to match every dependent clause with an independent clause to avoid creating a sentence fragment.

RELATIVE CLAUSES

Relative clauses are dependent clauses whose subjects are always either *who*, *whom*, *that*, or *which*. Always use *who* or *whom* to refer to people, unless your intention is to insult someone by referring to him or her as an inanimate object. Use *who* if the pronoun is serving as the subject of the clause; otherwise use *whom*. The distinction between *that* and *which* is commonly ignored these days. But to be technically correct, use *that* for restrictive relative clauses and *which* for non-restrictive clauses.

Restrictive relative clauses restrict the meaning of the sentence; non-restrictive clauses do not. For instance, the sentence, *I am going to sell the condo that I bought last summer*, contains the restrictive relative clause, *that I bought last summer*. Notice that this is a dependent clause; it cannot stand meaningfully on its own. It also restricts the meaning to indicate which of my several condos I will sell: the one I bought last summer, not the one I bought last autumn. If the purpose is not to help me refine the condo reference but simply to add extra information about it, then I would write, *I am going to sell the condo, which I bought last summer*. Notice that I not only substituted *which* for *that*, more importantly, I inserted a comma before the pronoun. You can think of non-restrictive clauses as being extra information that you could perhaps place in parenthesis but are instead setting off with a comma. For instance, I could have written instead, I *am going to sell the condo (which I bought last summer)*.

Sometimes the distinction is subtle between whether the meaning should be restricted or not, and often the choice of whether to punctuate a relative clause as restrictive or not-restrictive may not be significant. But there are important instances, especially in contracts and legal documents**, where the inclusion or omission of the comma literally defines the meaning of an agreement.** So in those circumstances it especially pays to think about whether you have properly punctuated the relative clause.

Because sentences sometimes contain several clauses, you must also ensure that every clause contains a matching subject and verb. If it does not, a sentence fragment will result. So always check to see that every subject has a verb. For instance, the phrase, *The banker who approved my loan*, is a sentence fragment because no verb accompanies *banker*, which ought to be the subject of the independent clause. The subject of the verb *approved* is the relative pronoun *who*; so *who approved my loan* is a complete clause. But it is a relative clause, which means it is a dependent clause that needs to link to an independent clause. However, none exists here because there is no verb accompanying *banker*. The reader still needs to know about the banker. What did he or she do? Lacking a verb, the phrase is matter without energy. So, in complex sentences that contain more than one clause, always be sure that every clause contains a matching subject and verb.

RELATIVE PRONOUNS

As I discussed above, relative clauses use special relative pronouns: *who*, *whom*, *that*, or *which*. Always use *who* or *whom* to refer to people. Use *who* for the subjective case, *whom* for the objective case, and *whose* for the possessive case (not *who's*, which always means *who is*). Thus we might write, **She** [singular subjective case] *praised* **them** [plural objective case] *for giving* **their** [plural possessive case] *seats to the pregnant women* **who** [plural subjective relative pronoun for humans] *had just boarded the bus,* **which** [singular, subjective, non-restrictive relative pronoun for inanimate things] *was going to the hospital.*

COMMON GRAMMATICAL ERRORS

The most common grammatical errors stem from mismatches between subjects and verbs. These include sentence fragments, where either the subject or, more commonly, the verb is missing; run-on sentences, which lack the necessary punctuation for separating independent clauses, and improper subject–verb agreement, where the writer has paired a singular verb form with a plural subject (noun), or vice-versa. Errors in parallel structure, errors forming the possessive case, and improper noun–pronoun agreement are other common problems. ***If you can understand and eliminate these six basic errors, you will eliminate the vast majority of grammatical problems within your writing.***

SENTENCE FRAGMENTS

Sentence fragments typically occur when writers fail to link a dependent clause to an independent clause, as discussed above, or when they omit the verb. For instance, *First-in, First-Out accounting procedures* is a sentence fragment by itself. It presents a concept but does not state anything about it. It is matter without energy. The best way to check for such errors when you are proofreading is to ask yourself for every sentence, *What is the verb?* In the *First-In, First-Out* example no verb is present; so the phrase is a fragment.

Whenever you cannot locate a verb, you have written a fragment. In those instances, you will need to rework the sentence to include a verb. Sometimes this will require you to think more deeply about what you really mean or what your point is. In other words, fragmentation of sentences often occurs when writers fail to formulate their thoughts completely. This represents another instance where we can see a close connection between solid, disciplined thinking and strong writing.

RUN-ON SENTENCES

Run-on sentences typically result from improper punctuation. A sentence (independent clause) is the smallest complete unit of thought. We use a period to indicate when that unit of thought is finished, unless we merge it with other clauses.

Rules of punctuation govern how we merge sentences. For instance, when linking a dependent clause to an independent clause, place a comma between them: *Because I scored well on the aptitude test, the committee selected me as a candidate for the open position.* If the two clauses are short and simple, many writers will omit the comma; so you have some leeway in the use of this comma in such situations: *Because I was hungry I ate lunch.* Or, *I was elated after we won*.

The most common error occurs when two sentences are joined by a conjunction (*and*, *or*, *but*). In those instances, you should precede the conjunction with a comma. Omitting the comma creates a run-on sentence—also known as a "comma splice." Note the proper placement of the comma in the following sentence in which the conjunction *but* joins two independent clauses: *We should diversify our foreign holdings, but we should consolidate our domestic assets.*

We can also use semicolons to merge independent clauses that either are not linked by transitional phrases or that use coordinating adverbs such as *thus, therefore, however, moreover, furthermore, otherwise, so,* and *hence.* Note the placement of the semicolon and the comma in the following sentence: *Miami is fabulous during the winter; the humidity drops, and the temperature cools down.* You can always replace a semicolon with a period and create two separate, complete sentences: *Miami is fabulous during the winter. The humidity drops, and the temperature cools down.* However, because the two clauses are short and closely related, you can link them with a semicolon instead. (The comma and the conjunction *and* link two, short independent clauses: *The humidity drops, and the temperature cools down.*) You should use semicolons to merge sentences only when they are closely related conceptually; otherwise, you will be hinting at a stronger relationship between them than really exists. Semicolons are among the most frequently abused marks of punctuation; so when in doubt, place a period and create two sentences.

As stated above, you may use semicolons to merge independent clauses where one of the clauses begins with a coordinating adverb. For example, consider the sentence, *I planned to write the report yesterday; however a power failure shut down my computer.* I have joined two independent clauses with the coordinating adverb, *however.* I could have written this as two, free-standing sentences: *I planned to write the report yesterday. However a power failure shut down my computer.* But writing the idea as a single sentence allows me to emphasize the close relationship between the clauses. Like subordinators, coordinating adverbs show logical relationships. But unlike subordinators, they do not create dependent clauses. A clause beginning with a subordinator cannot stand alone. By itself, ***Although** a power failure shut down my computer* is a sentence fragment. But a clause beginning with coordinator can stand alone: ***However** a power failure shut down my computer* is a complete sentence.

Semicolons are completely unrelated to colons. They are not half-hearted colons. Many people seem afraid to use a full colon, so they use a semicolon instead. That is just wishy washy punctuation. Never, for example, introduce a short list with a semicolon. Use a full colon instead, such as in the following sentence. A secretary has many responsibilities*:* typing, filing, answering the phone, and greeting customers. Use colons, not semicolons, for lists.

SUBJECT - VERB AGREEMENT

Subject–verb agreement is an easy concept, but errors abound nonetheless. Most people have no problem pairing singular verb forms with singular subjects, and plural verb forms with plural subjects, when the subject and verb fall next to each other in the sentence. Few people write, The **broker invest** in stocks instead of The **broker invests** in stocks, or The **students goes** to college instead of The **students go** to college. But when several words separate the subject from the verb, problems sometimes ensue. In the sentence, *A truckload of wood chips cost six hundred dollars*, I have improperly established agreement between the plural noun *chips* and the verb beside it, *cost*. However, the actual subject of the sentence is *truckload*, a singular noun; not *chips*. So I need a singular verb form, *costs*, to agree with the singular subject, even though the subject is separated from the verb by an intervening phrase. Thus, the sentence should read, *A truckload of wood chips costs six hundred dollars*. Notice that I could delete *of wood chips* and the sentence would still make sense: *A truckload costs six hundred dollars*. But deleting *A truckload* renders the sentence meaningless: *Of wood chips cost six hundred dollars*.

Relative clauses can separate subjects and verbs by great distances. I have placed in bold face the relative clause in the following sentence: *The institutions **that historically have had the greatest impact on the national economy** yield consistently solid returns on investment*. The independent clause is, *The institutions yield consistently solid returns on investment.* Even though the subject of that independent clause, *institutions*, is separated from the verb, *yield*, by a long relative clause, and even though *yield* appears beside a singular noun, *economy*, I must still make the agreement between the plural subject, *institutions*, and the main verb. Thus I choose *yield* instead of *yields*. For every clause you should be able to identify which subject goes with which verb.

PARALLEL STRUCTURE

When you present a list or sequence of activities, all of the items must be the same part of speech. For instance, in the sentence, *Let's **eat**, **drink**, and **be** merry*, all of the activities are simple verbs. In the sentence, ***Writing**, **drawing**, **gardening**, and **playing** tennis are my favorite pastimes*, all of the items are present participles. Present participles are verb forms that serve as nouns, and they end in *ing*.

Errors occur when the items in the list are not the same part of speech. For instance, ***Writing**, **drawing**, **to garden**, and **to play** tennis are my favorite pastimes* mixes present participles (*writing* and *drawing*) with infinitives, which are also verb forms that serve as nouns but which always begin with *to* (*to garden*, *to play*). To be grammatically correct the sentence must use either all participles or all infinitives. Failure to do so distorts the parallel structure within the sentence.

THE POSSESSIVE CASE

It is probably a toss-up over which is the most frequently abused punctuation mark: the semicolon or the apostrophe. We use the apostrophe to merge two words into one (contractions) and to show possession. Examples of contractions include *it's* instead of *it is*; *I'll* instead of *I shall*; *you'll* instead of *you will*; *they're* instead of *they are*; and *can't* instead of *cannot*. When used to show possession, the apostrophe can always be replaced by the phrase, *of the*. Thus *the account of the client* substitutes for *the client's account*. Notice that using the apostrophe in this case produces a smoother, less wordy sentence; so normally I recommend using the apostrophe instead of *of the*, except for when it seems awkward to do so.

We show the possessive by affixing *'s* to the end of a noun. We never use an apostrophe to show the possessive in a pronoun. In particular, the possessive form of *it* is *its*, not *it's*. This is a very common error. **It's always means *it is*.** To form the possessive of a plural noun, affix *'s*, unless the word ends in *s*, as many plural nouns do. Thus we restate *the shoes of the men* as *the men's shoes*. But if the plural form of the noun ends in *s*, just affix the apostrophe and omit the final *s*. Thus *payments by the clients* becomes *the clients' payments*. (Technically, if the plural noun ending in *s* is only one syllable, you should affix the full *'s*. For instance, *the laces of the shoes* becomes the *shoes's laces*. However, that seems picky to me, and certainly no clarity of meaning is lost if you omit the final *s* and write *shoes'.* The meaning would still refer to the laces of two or more shoes. If you meant the laces of only one shoe, you would place the apostrophe before the final *s*: *the shoe's laces*.)

Never use the apostrophe to form the simple plural; just add an *s* to most single nouns. It is alarming how often this error appears on billboards, in brochures, and in public documents. *We have several **options** before us* is correct. *We have several **option's** before us* is incorrect.

NOUN - PRONOUN AGREEMENT AND OTHER PRONOUN-RELATED ISSUES

Noun–Pronoun agreement is similar to Subject–Verb agreement. Replace a singular noun with a singular pronoun and a plural noun with a plural pronoun: *A truckload...**it**; wood chips...**they***. This is true no matter how many words intervene between the noun and pronoun.

Ambiguous pronouns are one of the greatest sources of confusion in writing; so, if many words intervene, you may not want to use a pronoun at all. It is essential that there be no likely way for the reader to think the pronoun refers to one noun when you want it to refer to another. So be attentive to this. **Whenever you use a pronoun, be sure there is only one possible noun to which it can refer.** It is especially essential to avoid ambiguous pronouns in contracts and other legal documents that specify the obligations of and remuneration for each party.

Consider, for instance, the following sentences: *Financial institutions are important to the fiscal well-being of small businesses. When they experience difficulties, the marketplace becomes unstable.* To what noun does *they* refer? Certainly, my meaning becomes very different if I intend for it to refer to *financial institutions* instead of *small businesses*. Both nouns are plural, and while *they* is closer to *businesses*, it has the same grammatical function as *institutions*—both function as subjects. So using *they* in this situation would be unacceptable because its meaning would be ambiguous; it can refer to more than one noun.

In this case it would be best to use another noun instead of *they*. For instance, I could write, *Financial institutions are important to the fiscal well-being of small businesses.* ***When banks and other lending agencies*** *experience difficulties, the marketplace becomes unstable.* If you cannot think of a different noun to replace the initial one, then repeat the initial one. Repetition is always better than ambiguity, even if it renders the prose stylistically awkward. So rather than use the ambiguous *they*, it is preferable to write, **Financial institutions** *are important to the fiscal* *well-being of small businesses. When **financial institutions** experience difficulties, the marketplace becomes unstable.*

Sometimes writers fail to precede them with any noun at all. For instance, in the previous sentence, to what noun does *them* refer? Presumably it refers to *pronouns*, but I have not even used that word for several sentences. So all I have done is to confuse my readers. You should always be able to identify a specific noun that is replaced by each pronoun.

Avoid using *this* as a pronoun. Sometimes this practice poses no problem. If I write, *Keep good records. This will help you run your business better*, no confusion arises. *This* obviously refers to the practice of keeping good records, and no harm comes from employing it in such a fashion. But do not use *this* to refer to anything more abstract than this example.

Sometimes writers will allude to the content of an entire paragraph with *this*. That practice is too vague and can lead to ambiguity or confusion. Too often, writers hide behind imprecisely defined terms like *this* when they, themselves, are not clear about what they mean. So, in most cases, treat *this* as the adjective it is, not as a noun. Doing so will compel you to be precise. Even in the example above, I could have easily written, *Keep good records. This practice will help you run your business better*. In this revision I am using *this* as an adjective to modify the noun *practice*, and I have thereby made my writing more concrete and more precise.

GENDER-NEUTRAL PRONOUNS

The English language has no gender-free singular pronoun that can be applied to people. *It,* unfortunately, refers only to non-human things, and *they*, which is gender-free, refers only to plural nouns. Until the 1970s, the established convention replaced singular nouns with the masculine pronoun (*he, him, his*), if the gender of the antecedent noun could be either male or female. Thus the earlier convention would have had us write, *The student. . .he; the employee. . .he; the executive. . .he;* and *the embezzler. . .he.*

Since the 1970s, however, this convention has been criticized for excluding women from how we think about each of these nouns. For instance, if we always replace *manager* or *CEO* with *he* and never with *she*, all users of the language, both male and female, will instinctively tend to think of managers and CEOs as male, unless they make a special effort not to. Thus, just through regular usage, *manager* and *CEO* would become masculine nouns, like *father, brother,* or *son*—words that can refer only to males. And this association would carry over into our behavior. When it becomes time to look for new managers or CEOs, men would be at a competitive advantage, because the decision-makers would already be associating these executive positions with men without even thinking about it. Of course, the practice can work against men as well if, for instance, we always refer to *the criminal. . .he,* or the *power-crazed maniac. . .he* .

Because I believe in the power of language to shape our perception, and because several women have told me how, as girls, they grew up feeling apart from groups and occupations that were routinely described with masculine pronouns, I believe the criticisms of the old convention are valid. Unfortunately, no satisfactory alternative convention has risen in its place. *He/she*, *he or she*, and *s/he* are awkward and distracting. And it is unacceptable to use *they* to replace a singular noun, as that violates noun-pronoun agreement and may create confusion or ambiguity.

In many cases the best way to address this problem is to use a plural noun in the first place, if you can, and then replace it with the gender-neutral plural pronoun *they* (or *them* or *their* in the objective and possessive cases). For instance, you can replace, *The manager must sign his or her name in black ink* with, *Managers must sign their names in black ink*. This is an effective strategy when the meaning and structure of the sentence will permit it.

Sometimes, however, the singular noun is necessary. In those cases, each writer must decide for herself or himself how to deal with this problem. You may wish to write *he or she* the first time you use the pronouns to replace a particular noun, and after that use only one of the pronouns to avoid the awkwardness of having to write *he or she* seven or eight times on a single page. If you decide to do that, be sure to retain the same pronoun throughout. In other words, on the repeated uses always use *he* or always use *she*, but do not alternate them, as this will create confusion. For instance, if describing how to treat a particular patient of unknown gender, it would be inappropriate to use the plural, *patients*. Instead you might write, *Ask the patient if his or her stomach has been upset. If yes, then ask her if she has eaten anything unusual in the past three days. If no, then ask her if she has had trouble breathing, and then if she has experienced any soreness in her muscles.*

However you decide to handle this situation, consider not just your own personal beliefs about the issue, but also those of your readers. Remember, it is important always to anticipate your readers' responses. So if you think using *he* to replace all references to managers or CEOs will alienate the readers of your report, then it is not worth it to choose that word. Remember, you want your readers to respond to the content of what you are saying, and not to whether your word choice is somehow offensive or alienating. So choosing words that will provoke or distract your readers is always counterproductive in business and analytical writing, unless for some reason your intention is to upset them.

CHAPTER 7
STYLE

When we speak of writing style, we usually refer to the tone, diction, use of active and passive voice verbs, and the rhythms of the prose. Strong writing uses styles that are concise, precise, crisp, and direct.

TONE

Strong professional writing usually employs a serious, straightforward tone that is formal without being stiff or awkward in its formality. Irony, flippancy, and sarcasm are inappropriate for two excellent reasons. First, their tone is unprofessional. Second, these are usually subtle forms of expression. Without the accompanying vocal inflections and facial gestures available in speech, written irony and sarcasm can easily be missed, in which case your reader will take seriously something you intended to ridicule. This defeats the entire purpose of your writing, and being clever just is not worth that. So, in an academic or professional environment, it is always best to play it straight in your writing.

You can achieve a serious tone by avoiding slang and undignified jargon and by taking each sentence seriously and striving to make it complete, grammatically correct, accurate, precise, and concise. Getting directly to the point and never digressing unnecessarily from it will also give your writing a professional sensibility. You should be polite and respectful without becoming a sycophant. Give your readers the respect they deserve, but do not overdo it.

DICTION

Diction, or word choice, plays a significant role in strong writing. By choosing exactly the right nouns and verbs, you can often eliminate adjectives and adverbs and thereby be more concise and often more precise. For instance, we can replace *The athlete **ran very fast** to the finish line* with *The athlete **raced** to the finish line*. The meanings of both sentences are identical, but the second one is more concise and employs a more dynamic verb. You can always replace *due to the fact that* with *because* or *due to*.

Choosing strong verbs is the single best way to create a strong writing style. It is not always possible to do so in every sentence, but, as discussed in the previous chapter, as much as possible you should place the real weight of the meaning on verbs instead of nouns or adjectives. For instance, in the sentence, *There are many clients who prefer to be billed quarterly*, the verb in the main clause, *are*, is one of the weakest verb choices possible. *Prefer* is a much stronger verb. Rewriting the sentence, *Many clients prefer to be billed quarterly*, or even *Many clients prefer quarterly billings*, not only reduces the total number of words by nearly 50 percent, without losing any clarity or meaning, it also creates a more dynamic sentence, one whose main verb conveys the most important concept in the sentence: the clients' preference.

Bureaucratic language often robs sentences of their vitality by turning verbs into nouns. For instance, a bureaucrat might rewrite the dynamic and efficient, *Company X acquired Company Y* as, *The acquisition of Company Y was made by Company X*. The wordy rewrite gains no additional clarity. It places the weight of the meaning on a noun, *acquisition*, instead of on a verb, *acquired*, and it sacrifices the active voice verb *acquired* for the passive voice verb phrase, *was made*.

ACTIVE AND PASSIVE VOICE VERBS

The grammatical difference between active and passive voice centers on the subject of the sentence. In an active voice construction, the performer of the action is both the grammatical and conceptual subject of the verb. Thus in the active voice sentence, *The agent closed the deal*, *agent* is both the grammatical subject of the verb *closed* as well as the conceptual subject. It is the agent who is doing the closing. In the passive voice construction, *The deal was closed by the agent*, the agent is still the conceptual subject—he or she is still closing the deal. However, *agent* no longer functions as the grammatical subject, which is now *deal*.

Thus passive voice shifts focus away from the conceptual subject. Indeed, the passive voice makes it possible to remove the conceptual subject from the sentence altogether. *The deal was closed* is a complete and grammatically correct, passive voice sentence. But notice that the conceptual subject—the person who closed the deal—is entirely missing. Proper uses of the passive voice do exist, and not all applications of the passive voice result in stylistic flaws. Sometimes we do not know who committed the action; so we have no choice but to employ the passive voice. But far too often it merely results in a wordy, indirect, and unnecessarily weak statement.

One way to help spot passive voice verbs is to check to see if a helping verb has been included. Not every helping verb creates the passive voice, but all passive constructions use helping verbs. In the example above, *was closed* is the complete verb phrase: *closed* is the main verb and *was* is the helping verb. Helping verbs are always verbs of being, typically: *is*, *are*, *was*, and *were*.

A common but reprehensible use of the passive voice, especially in bureaucratic institutions, is to avoid assigning responsibility for an action. We may learn that the deal was closed, but we don't know whom to reward or blame. For this reason, the passive voice often becomes a tool in office politics. While it may offer some short term advantage to individuals and departments that hide behind intentional vagueness, in the long run this practice harms the executive's ability to manage effectively, because the passive voice obscures accountability, such as when someone writes, *Mistakes were made.* For this reason alone, top executives should insist that employees use the active voice as much as possible.

In conclusion, language both reflects and helps create our perceptions of reality. This is the main reason why active voice verbs usually perform better than passive ones. People who use the active voice reflect a reality in which individuals and agencies do things, whereas people who employ the passive voice reflect a reality in which things are somehow done.

RHYTHM

Orchestrating the rhythms of the language is a practice for more advanced writers. People who are still struggling to make their sentences say exactly what they mean should not concern themselves with the music of their prose. But it is a nice refinement. A report whose language flows smoothly and comfortably is more pleasant to read than one that proceeds in jerks and starts. You can alter the rhythms by using parallel structures, repeating certain types of phrases, and even by choosing one equivalent word instead of another when the first has a vocal stress pattern that falls easier on the ear.

Varying sentence structures is another way to shape the rhythm of your writing. (Notice the difference in sound between the previous sentence and "...is another way to shape your *writing's rhythm*." Both mean the same thing, but they do not feel the same.) If you have several short sentences in a row, you could follow them with a longer sentence to break up the pace. If you are reciting a list of facts, you can find ways to merge sentences in order to avoid having a choppy-sounding string of short, declarative sentences. Beginning sentences with dependent clauses not only highlights logical relationships, it also varies sentence patterns. (You will recall that these clauses begin with subordinators such as *because*, *since*, *although*, *if*, *when*, etc.) There are other ways you can alter your sentence constructions so that not every clause reads Subject–Verb–Object. But remember, never sacrifice clarity of meaning for enhanced style.

EXERCISES

Rewrite the following sentences more efficiently and correct all grammatical errors. There are several correct ways to revise these sentences, and I provide sample revisions on the next page.

1. Due to the fact that we will be testing the new operations system, the computers' will be down on Friday, August 15, from 8:30 to 3:30 P.M.

2. The account will be handled by our most senior partner.

3. By using the new software package accounting procedures will be simplified.

4. Through supply and demand the market is made to fluctuate.

5. In this report I will explain the significance of the research project I am presently taking part in, as well as some of the steps that will be taken to complete the project.

6. Implementing the new system involves completing a preliminary feasibility study, doing an environmental impact study, a cost analysis, the completion of a survey of the users, and to train the personnel who will use the system.

7. I will explain how the computer program translates data inputted by the

engineers, creating a model that is tested by the engineer.

8. I will not be able to say with exactitude whether or not we will be using the new system or the old one.

9. The last person to sign-off on the project, who has the ultimate authority and who is given the greatest reward at the end of the year, if the project is successful.

10. Each of the technicians should take his or her tools with him or her when a piece of equipment is going to be serviced by him or her.

SAMPLE REVISIONS

1. Because we will be testing the new operations system, the computers will be down on Friday, August 15, from 8:30 A.M. to 3:30 P.M. [*Because* replaces *due to the fact that*, and I have added *A.M.* where it was omitted.]

2. Our most senior partner will handle the account. [The new sentence uses active voice instead of passive voice.]

3. The new software will simplify our accounting procedures. [The new sentence uses active voice instead of passive voice.]

4. The market fluctuates due to supply and demand. OR
   Supply and demand make the market fluctuate.

5. In this report I will explain the significance of my project and some steps I will take to complete it.

6. Implementing the new system involves completing a preliminary feasibility study, doing an environmental impact study, analyzing costs, surveying users, and training the personnel who will oversee the system. [I have rewritten the sentence to preserve parallel structure. Here each item in the list of activities is the same part of speech—in this case a present participle.]

7. I will explain how the computer program uses the engineers' data to create a model they can test.

8. I cannot say with certainty whether we will use the old system or the new one.

9. The last person to sign-off on the project has the ultimate authority and receives the greatest reward at the end of the year, if it is successful. [The original version is a sentence fragment, as no verb accompanies *last person*.]

10. All the technicians should take their tools when they are going to service a piece of equipment. [I have replaced the passive voice *is going to be serviced* with the active voice *they are going to service*, and I have eliminated the need for a singular pronoun caused by the use of *each* in the original sentence, thereby eliminating the awkwardness of repeating *his or her* and *him or her.* Be aware that *each* and *every* always take singular verb forms and singular pronouns. For instance, it is correct to write, *Every worker **receives** a bonus at the end of the year in **his or her** paycheck.* It would be a violation of pronoun agreement to write *Every worker **receive**. . .in **their** paycheck.*]

CHAPTER 8
PROOFREADING

As T.S. Eliot writes, *In my end is my beginning.* I thus conclude this book where I started: discussing rigorous, disciplined thinking. More than anything else, proofreading involves comparing what you want to communicate with what you have actually written. Wherever discrepancies occur, you must alter your writing until you are completely satisfied that you have truly expressed what you mean.

After you have completed writing your essay or report, change your role from writer to reader and approach your work as a reasonable but critical reader. You do not want to insist on unnecessary details and qualifications when they are not required to make your meaning clear. However, you do need to look out for any places where a reasonable reader might conceivably misunderstand you, or require more information, or have difficulty following your logic or train of thought. Keep the needs of your specific readers in mind, and be particularly attentive to ambiguous phrases and ambiguous pronouns. These can completely alter your meaning, sometimes in plausible ways. The disastrous possibilities here are obvious, and no one can be held at fault but the writer.

Too often novice writers equate proofreading with checking for spelling and typographical errors. (With Spellcheck on almost every word processor, there is no excuse for most spelling errors.) But while those are important, especially as misspelled and mistyped words detract from a professional appearance, they are secondary compared to satisfying yourself that the writing truly achieves its purpose. That arrangement of priorities should seem obvious, but it is astounding how often people spend more time worrying about the paper's appearance than its content. Worry about both, but worry about content more. After all, the content is the reason why you wrote the piece in the first place and why the reader has bothered to read it.

You can train yourself to be a good proofreader by getting in the habit of questioning yourself as you read your work. It is a good idea to proofread everything at least twice. I typically proofread my work five or six times.

On the first pass read for overall continuity and obvious errors and typos. Does the writing generally seem to achieve its purpose? Do you begin with a strong thesis statement that truly lays out the entire discussion? Do you deliver the promises you make at the beginning in terms of what the essay or report will provide? Are main points clear? Does each paragraph begin with an effective topic sentence? Does the writing seem focused, or does it wander from point to point? Can you identify the overall structure of the discussion? Is it written at the appropriate level for your readers?

Once you are satisfied about the big picture, scrutinize each individual sentence on a second reading. Does every sentence say exactly what you mean? Are there ambiguities or misleading statements? Have you used the active voice? If not, can you now rewrite the sentence more effectively with an active voice verb? Is the sentence grammatically correct? Are the words properly spelled? Is the logical connection apparent between this sentence and the ones preceding and following it? Are there any implications to this statement that you have not considered? If you have made numerous changes on your second reading, go over it a third time. Keep going over it until you have made an entire pass without further corrections. Since it is always easier to spot someone else's errors than your own, if it is an especially important document, try to have someone else read it after you have completed your own proofreading.

With this intense scrutiny of your own work, you will rest assured that no one else has thought more carefully about your writing than you have; consequently, you will be less likely to encounter unexpected criticism. You will also be sharpening your analytic thinking skills, since the same set of questions you use to challenge yourself can apply to how you evaluate the quality of other people's thoughts. These practices will help you identify flaws with their thinking and thus enable you to avoid perpetuating their errors. You may very likely develop a reputation for being a sharp thinker, which is a good reputation to have in a business or academic environment.

All of these practices can build greater self-confidence, which in turn leads to better performance and higher achievement. But it requires the discipline discussed in Chapter One. Virtually anyone can become a strong writer and strong thinker. You need only to demand quality from yourself at all times and to push yourself beyond superficial inspection of your thoughts to real, probing, rigorous self-scrutiny. *Know thyself*, says the Delphic Oracle from ancient Greece. Such is the path to strength.